The Backyard Roosters of Saint Paul

Written and Illustrated
By
Susan Gainen

The Small Friends' Research Institute
2015

Find more of Susan Gainen's art and writing at
www.susangainenartist.com

Original art, prints, and downloadable projects
https://www.etsy.com/shop/SusanGainen

Creatures and abstracts on cool products
http://www.zazzle.com/susangainen

Creatures and abstracts on Fabric & Wallpaper
http://www.spoonflower.com/profiles/susangainen

Follow me on Twitter @PTBSusanGainen
"Like" **https://www.facebook.com/susangainenartist**

The 52 images in this book are for sale.
Contact me for originals, prints, or other products:
susangainen@comcast.net - 651.917.0219

Thanks to
The Small Friends Research Institute
Tall Cat Productions

TABLE OF CONTENTS

The Small Friends' Research Institute

In August 2011, through collaboration among a Flight of Fancy, a Gift of Imagination, and a generous gift from the LLLama Families, the Small Friends' Research Institute opened its doors for research into previously overlooked whimsical creatures.

Since then, Institute researchers identified dozens of creatures and species including The Competitive Frog Teams, Friendly Dragons, the creatures in the Lost Cave Paintings of Saint Paul, the Pandas & Frogs of the Hidden Bamboo Forest of Saint Paul, and Wild Parrots of the Grim Winter of 2013. More work needs to be done with these, and the search for additional evidence of modern, historic, and pre-historic whimsy will continue.

Publications in 2012. The Institute published *The Small Friends' Chronicles*, a 70-page compendium of whimsical creatures' portraits and stories. (softcover, ebook, jpg). After the LLLama Families graciously donated their archives (which were a mess), Institute researchers found 29 portraits and stories, published *Meet the LLLamas* (softcover & e-book).

The Institute's Executive Director and SpokesCat is The Tall Cat. He works tirelessly to create new research opportunities for the sadly neglected field of Global Whimsical History. He is also on the Board of *More Whimsy Before Breakfast*, a non-profit whose prime directive is neatly summarized in its name.

Why Roosters?

When my doctor urges me to do more exercise, I point out that I exercise my imagination every day. He is not amused.

Why Roosters? Or, the better question: Why birds?

As a Whimsical Wildlife Documentarian, the opportunity to exercise my imagination with birds is too good to pass up. Think of it. They have feathers of all colors and sizes, eyes, beaks, claws, and an astonishing array of body shapes which are all good springboards for imagination, creativity, and Pure Whimsy.

Since 2010, I have painted birds from the Lost Cave Paintings of Saint Paul (two Do-Dos, owls, parrots, peacocks, penguins, propeller-tails, and The Grand Cave Toucan), Sophie the Opera Bird, Flightless Flora (a fortunate match-up between a flamingo and a trademarked floor mop, noted on her birth certificate as "Father: Hearty Floor Mop"), Bessie the Bead-Bellied Block Feather, dozens of hummingbirds, flocks of owls, oh so many parrots, a pheasant, a Spoonbill, cardinals, ducks, flocks of flamingos (including the *acapella* group "3 Cats & 11 Flamingos"), The Feminist Hens Leaving the Henhouse, and a few extinct or perhaps purely imaginary birds.

And roosters. Lots of roosters. The Backyard Roosters of Saint Paul challenge me to make them as brightly colored as they are in "life." Some have opened doors to new techniques, papers, and mediums. Always, they astonish me with their stories.

My Prime Directive is to Spread Whimsy, and The Backyard Roosters of Saint Paul always want to lead that parade.

The First Roosters

red rooster 1
srapainen 4.07

I used a tiny sushi cutter to trace these tiny roosters, and a double-zero brush to paint inside the lines.

Robert
The Tap Dancing Rooster

Robert was the first character to make noise in my studio. He had become obsessed with tap dancing (which he demonstrated), and tapped until 2 am.

When he was no longer interested in crowing at dawn, in a surprising act of Hen House democracy, the hens booted him out of the House.

Robert tap dances 'til 2 a.m. He does not crow at dawn.

Robert the Tap Dancing Rooster

He came to me for a portrait and for career counseling. Now he is on his way to being named the First Tap Dancing Rooster* on Broadway.

In the musical "Annie," the character of Rooster Harrigan is played by a human.

Cousin Charlie #2 and Friends

Cousin Charlie #2

Red Charlie

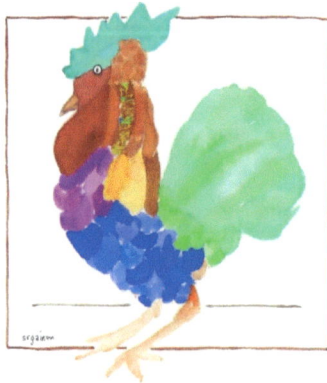

Rainbow Charlie

There are many Cousin Charlies in the Backyards of Saint Paul. Each is proud of his feathers and wants to lead the Rooster Parade. That's why there are three Rooster Parades every single day.

Cousin Charlie #3

Cousin Charlie #3   Charlie Blue

Cousin Charlie #3 and his cousin Charlie Blue are best friends. They are fond of blue food, and eat as often as possible at their pal Blue Dot LLLama's restaurant, "My Blues Heaven and Potato Palace." The menu***** includes:

Blue corn and blue cheese quesadillas	Blueberry & blue corn muffins
Blueberry & blue corn pancakes	Blue Potato Shepherd's Pie
Blueberry Pie	Blueberry Buckle
Blueberry Crisp	Blue Crab Cakes
Cooked Poppy Seed Milkshakes	Blue Curacao-based drinks
Blue Mashed Potato Bar	Blueberry Wine
Blueberry Chili Chutney	Blue Corn Chips

*As explained in *Meet the LLLamas*, a compendium of LLLama Families' portraits and stories.

Cousin Charlie #4

Cousin Charlie #4, the lawyer in this extended family, is often quoted in the *Daily Rooster Review*, and he publishes frequently in *The Gallus Gazette*, the journal of record of the Rooster business.

He is planning a Kick (Crow) Starter campaign to create an international journal of Rooster Law and Litigation.

The French Rooster

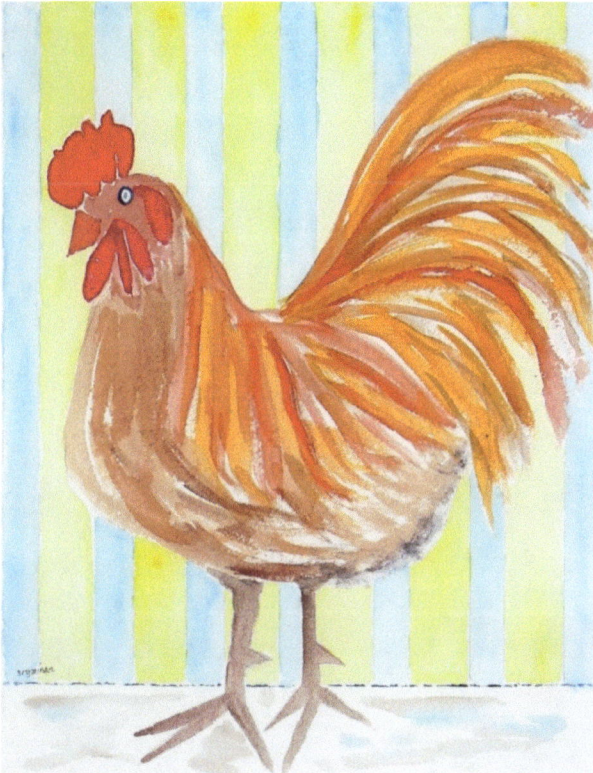

Among the first roosters to visit my studio, French Rooster has a clear idea of his place in the world: "I want my image to be in every kitchen that has any of the works of Julia Child, The Goddess of French Cooking."

"Every kitchen?" I asked.

"You heard what I said. Every kitchen."

Bonita's Rooster

June Rooster spent a tiny amount of time in my studio. I took him for show-and-tell at my mystery book group and discovered that the hostess LOVED Roosters.

Knowing he'd have a good home, I left him there.

No collective noun for "rooster"

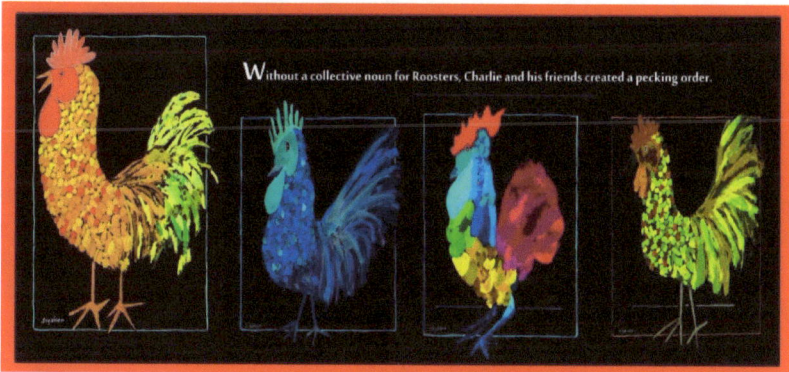

Without a collective noun for Roosters, Charlie and his friends created a pecking order.

Without a collective noun for "rooster," Charlie and his friends created a pecking order.

With a busy Rooster Parade schedule in Saint Paul (three a day), they change places every day. Fortunately, there are dozens of Roosters in Saint Paul willing to march for Rooster Glory.

Stained Glass Rooster #1

A lot of painted stained glass creatures have stopped by the studio. Many are in *The Small Friends' Chronicles*, a 70-page compendium of whimsical creatures' portraits and stories which also includes speculation about their origins.

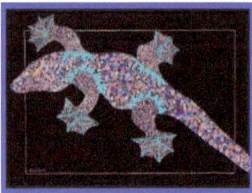

3 Roosters
Celebrate The 4th of July

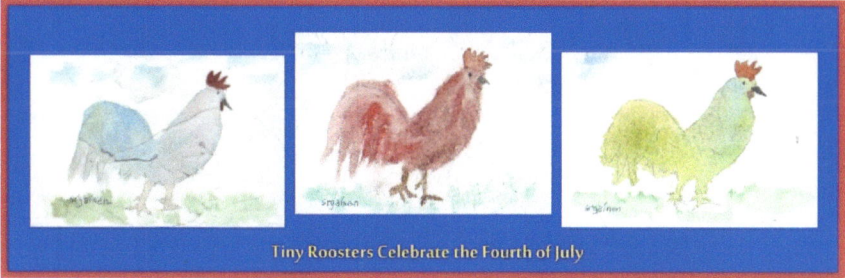

Tiny Roosters Celebrate the Fourth of July

July 4th is an important holiday in the Rooster and Hen calendar. It is marked by parades (a Rooster Favorite Activity), bright colors (if the sun is out), and very loud fireworks, which Roosters just adore.

They are less enthusiastic about the abundance of Fried Chicken consumed at picnics. They encourage barbecue (beef, pork, and game), fresh and smoked fish, tofu, all of the Pig Roast traditions, and the Vegetarian Option.

Not on their menus: Barbecued Chicken, Buffalo Wings, Chicken Apple Sausage, Chicken & Dumplings, Chicken Biryani, Chicken Corn Chowder, Chicken Enchiladas, Chicken Fingers, Chicken Fried Rice, Chicken Kiev, Chicken Larb, Chicken Marsala, Chicken Noodle Soup, Chicken Parmesan, Chicken Pho, Chicken Pot Pie, Chicken Quesadillas, Chicken Salad, Chicken With Cashews, Laurie Colwin's Amazing Mustard Chicken, Roast Chicken, and White Chicken Chili.

Red and Purple Rooster

Red is just proud to be a Rooster who would never, ever get lost in a crowd.

srgainen

Two Blue Rooster Cousins

Blue Bill and Blue Bob share a fondness for blue food, and they, too, frequent Blue Dot LLLama's "My Blues Heaven and Potato Palace."

They are big supporters of the public radio stations that play Bluegrass, Blues, and Jazz.

Tiny Cave Rooster
Lost Cave Paintings of Saint Paul

The Tiny Cave Rooster is one of many cave paintings made on 4x4-inch aluminum squares that are covered with tinted gesso and scrubbed to look like cave walls.

We know very little about what the spirits of the images in cave paintings do when we are not looking. Rumor has it that Tiny Rooster organizes races up and down stalagmites and stalactites. There is no confirmed evidence of this activity, but a majority of Avian Archeologists believe it.

More Tiny Cave Roosters
Lost Cave Paintings of Saint Paul

Minnesota is riddled with caves. Imagining and excavating the Lost Cave Paintings from the comfort of my living room studio is a pleasure. It is remarkably free of rats and bats, and I have no fear of cave-ins or arrests for trespass that might happen if I were in an actual Minnesota cave.

The Lost Rooster

The photograph contains explicit documentary evidence that this Rooster spent time on my easel. Note the very pale running cats (at left) that are in a painting that spent about two years on that easel, aging like Fine Wine (as opposed to Old Cheese).

This is the last I've seen of this Rooster. If you have seen him, say "Hi" for me.

3D Backyard Roosters: The Multi-Media Boys

Their backyard is tinted gesso. Each rooster is a separate cut-out and embellished bird.

The Boys are always on alert for entrepreneurial opportunities. Sometimes they work well, and sometimes they fail miserably. One notable catastrophe was their attempt to capitalize on Minnesota's turkey-growing industry, when they tried to convince watercolor artists to replace Kolinsky Sable Brushes with turkey feathers. Never!

3D Backyard Rooster
A Hybrid Bird

This portrait was meant to be all-painted-stained-glass, but the Rooster was a dud. Undeterred, and spurred on by the threat of rooster claws in my back, I cut and painted individual body, wattle, and coxcomb feathers, and applied them with acrylic mediums including glass bead gel. He is happy with this portrait.

3DBY is the Chief Executive Officer of *Gallus Minnesota*, which is dedicated to expanding Chicken Keeping throughout the state, and to preserving Minnesota's Chicken Culture.

Tiny Blue Backyard Rooster

Although a 36-inch-tall Rooster may be the Holy Grail of rooster breeding, Tiny Backyard Roosters will stand up to any Roosters for their variety, character, and charm. Tiny Blue is 4" tall.

Red Rooster From Hyperspace

My studio is a landing point for Creatures From Hyperspace. They stop for portraits, tell stories, and eat my snacks. These portraits are on a tree-free paper called TerraSkin™ (from Wet Paint in Saint Paul.) The paint looks like "hyperspace" because it puddles and dries instead of being absorbed as it would be on traditional papers.

Roosters Visit the Spa

Rooster Visitors 12/26/14

My studio has an exclusive Avian Spa Service. These Roosters stopped by for cleaning and rejuvenation, and to have some work done on their eyes.

They left with $700 worth of feather, skin, and eye-care products, and, because they are big tippers, the thanks of a grateful staff.

Two Shiny 3D Roosters

srgainen   2 shiny roosters-in-progress

These Roosters went through a complete Spa Treatment, which included re-touch of their paint, re-application of their acrylic mediums for super-shine, re-sharpening their claws, and reviving their eyes with my special blend of Avian Eye Revival Serum.™

Although they love the treatments and the products, they are reluctant to appear in spa advertising because they value their privacy.

Ready-to-Rock Rooster

A crew of Roosters participated in a 30-paintings-in-30-days challenge in January 2015. Ready-to-Rock is Number 5. He is always on the alert for live performance opportunities for his band, the Rockin' Roosters. Tweet him at **@RockinRoo**.

Glowing Rooster

srgainen

Glowing Rooster participated in the January 2015 30-paintings-in-30-days challenge. He had the good fortune of falling successfully through several Photoshop filters. He assures me that he is not radioactive.

Glowing Rooster works closely with astro-physicists who use some of his markings in their interstellar research projects.

3D Rooster and
Undercover 3D Rooster

After Undercover Rooster was encased in acrylic, he wandered into Photoshop, where his digital adventure was technically interesting but less than successful. He wants a do-over.

Curious Rooster

Curious Rooster has an overwhelming concern for cleanliness, and he pays particular attention to everything that falls onto the floor. Now retired, he spent part of his working life as an assistant in a tiny diamond jewelry studio. He always found the diamonds that fell on the floor, and didn't eat them. He has a special "Look! Look!" crow for fallen diamonds.

More than slightly obsessive, he collects bits of corn and sorts them by size. When he leads Rooster Parades, he makes everyone line up sorted by size and color.

Rooster #9
Meets Too Many
Photoshop Filters

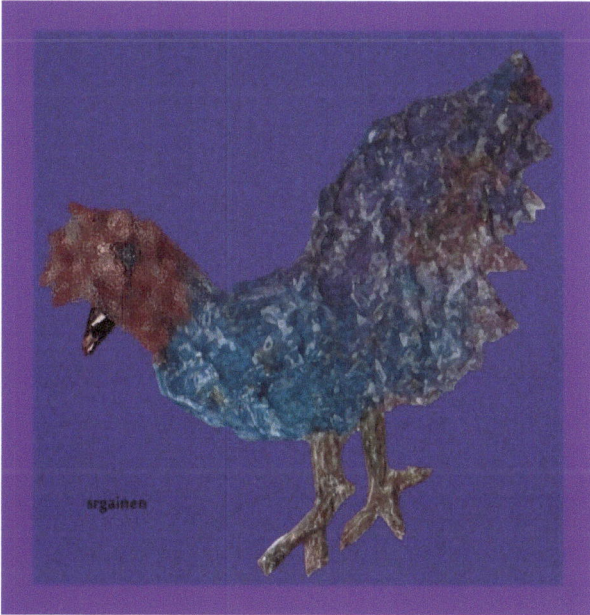

Rooster Number 9 from the 30-paintings-in-30-days challenge had a particularly unfortunate encounter with Photoshop filters. Close observers will be able to see three filters on the bird and one in the background.

He is not keen on his image and wants a do-over. Sadly, none are available.

Blue-Green Stained Glass Rooster

Happy to be part of the Painted Stained Glass family, Blue Green Rooster sits above the fray. He is more delicate than most, and he perches very high up in the Rooster Barn, focusing on his Tweets. He rarely crows.

Several branches of the Stained Glass creature families are joining with The Small Friends' Research Institute to document stained glass creatures in historic and contemporary artwork.

Stained Glass Hen (right) will lead this project. She is one of the first hens to leave the Hen House for work in the larger world.

Watcher
The Orange and Brown Rooster

Watcher, visible for only a few minutes each day, stands guard over the Backyard in a hidden location.

While predators are rare, there is a good deal of serious industrial espionage among Rooster Houses as they prepare their entries for Saint Paul's annual parades. The Winter Carnival, Grand Old Days, and Saint Patrick's Day parades are very important on the Rooster Calendar.

Marsala Rooster

Marsala Rooster celebrates both Old and New. He looks remarkably like a tin ceiling (old) and his color, Marsala, is the Pantone Color of 2015 (new).

Green Tail Rooster

Green Tail (G.T.) is an experienced political operative. He is the lobbyist for the Backyard Roosters of Saint Paul, the National Avian Protection Alliance, and the Gallus Division of the Audubon Society.

He has close ties to agencies monitoring international trafficking in endangered birds and ancient avian artifacts, and he is often called to testify in international avian criminal matters.

Winston Golden Boy Rooster

Winston's political ambitions are impossible to ignore. Even when he was a tiny cockerel (a young rooster), his leadership qualities brought his hatch mates together. He successfully organized literary societies, athletic events, and debating teams.

He is considering a run for the Avian Senate. He would like to be US President someday, but he is not optimistic about mounting a challenge to the Constitution to make that a possibility.

Piano Man Rooster

Piano Man Rooster was hatched in the backyard of some of Saint Paul's Human Piano Royalty. Mr. Piano is a beloved piano teacher and Mrs. Piano is one of the best jazz pianists in the country. Piano Man Rooster often tours with them.

Blue Crystal Rooster

Blue Crystal Rooster's family roots connect him with Roosters of Picasso's Blue and Cubist periods.

Their historic connection to French artists inspired the Museé D'Poulet, a collection of French and African art with rooster and hen images. It is near Sacha Finkelstein's Bakery and L'as Du Fallafal on Rue de Rosiers in Paris. See the art and stay for the excellent food.

Bright Fan Tail Rooster

Bright Fan Tail Rooster is a Fan Dancer. Human Fan Dancers are traditionally female, but they could learn a lot from Bright Fan, who has been practicing since his cockerel days.

His superb fan management and intricate foot work are admired throughout the Avian Dance World, and his classes are booked two years in advance.

About the Author

Susan Gainen is a Whimsical Wildlife Documentarian whose living room studio in Saint Paul, Minnesota, is on a flyway and path traveled by pre-historic, historic, contemporary, and purely imagined creatures.

They drop by to sit for portraits, tell their stories, and eat her snacks. Some just eat-and-run; others have stayed for years.

The first roosters arrived in 2007, and the most recent were part of a January 2015 30-paintings-in-30-days challenge. Although they have been banned from the Hen Houses by City Ordinance, all of the Roosters celebrate Saint Paul's Chicken-Keeping traditions. Good citizens, they live in neighborhood-friendly Rooster Palaces, which have high-tech-sound-insulated rehearsal halls for crowing practice.

She uses a variety of materials. Originally a watercolor purist, she was introduced to acrylic mediums in a WARM (Women's Art Resources of Minnesota) workshop in 2013. To her great delight, she learned about products that make paintings both shiny and bumpy (Gesso, Glass Bead Gel, Self-Leveling Clear Gel, and more).

All of her work is generously supported by The Small Friends' Research Institute, which is committed to expanding research into heretofore unknown and overlooked whimsical creatures.

All 52 of the images in this book are for sale in some form. Contact her at 651.917.0219, susangainen@comcast.net, or www.susangainenartist.com. She accepts commissions.

www.ingramcontent.com/pod-product-compliance
Lightning Source LLC
Chambersburg PA
CBHW040346060426

42445CB00029B/14